"Miracle Baby"

"Miracle Child"

Every day we live we learn more about society, this world, and ourselves. I knew some of my hiccups but I didn't understand the reason behind them. I was recently taught that due to my mom using drugs while pregnant with me, that not only did I have hard times breathing. I was born premature. I remember around 2 years of age, I was utilizing a breathing machine. I actually remember waking up in the middle of the night from shaking with my body filled with sweat. Not understanding at the time that I not only was I a premature baby, I was born addicted to drugs. My body was having withdrawals, which caused me to shake and sweat throughout the night. Hello my name is Darrell De'Mario Smith also known as Double D. As you may have read earlier, I was a "Crack Baby" as most would call it. For me to be writing this book, you can also call me a "Miracle Baby".

I grew up in Oakland California, 55th to be exact. I was blessed to be talented by the hands of GOD. I was always taught that GOD will bring people in your life to fulfill his purpose. At 6 months, my biological grandmother who was watching over me, took my older cousin to a local daycare. This particular day, GOD brought someone in all of our lives. When dropping my older cousin off to the day care provider, my grandmother asked if they would be kind to watch me as well. The daycare provider was very nice and said no problem. When my grandmother came back to get me and my older cousin Henry at the end of the day, the daycare provider knowing the circumstance of my mother being in and out of jail, on drugs, and my grandmother taking sick, said that she seen something in my eyes that connected her to me. At this present time my mom is serving some years behind bars due to a robbery and a drug charge. My grandmother who was watching over my cousin and I was sick internally but was still pushing with the grace of GOD. The daycare provider stated that she was able to make a home for me. Now I can't remember if my grandmother asked or if the daycare provider offered but long story short, this sweet lady saved my life. GOD sent Helen Raymond (Granny) to my life and grow me up to the man that I am today.

Granny took me in as one of her own children. She welcomed me with open arms. Her husband Emmett George Rhodes, was very understanding and open to trying this new adoption thing out. He would rock me to sleep at night with one eye open and one eye closed and just pat my back. They played a major role in me becoming a Father, Man of God, Business man, and a dominant figure. Now growing up with the title of being a foster kid wasn't easy but my granny never made me feel that I was adopted. They accepted me as their own and I never felt out of place. Every morning before school, my granny and I would say a prayer. This prayer would stay with me as a ritual forever. When my grandfather Emmett walked me to elementary, the kids would make fun of me due to knowing that he was my adopted grandfather. I became ashamed and started to fight a lot. This made me build anger issues and low self-esteem. Even after building up so much anger, that prayer that my granny prayed with me, stayed with me. I don't really

“Miracle Baby”

know what happened or why everything took place, but I do remember Emmett moving to Texas, my grandmother getting real ill and me being forced to move to West Oakland with my biological grandmother’s friend.

I don’t know where my granny was at the time but Lord knows I didn’t want to leave her. I was grateful to have a roof over my head, be clothed and cared for, but it was a big change for me. I remember I couldn’t ride my bike outside, so I rode it in the house. I began to feel alone with no friends and no family. I use to sit in the house and reminisce about when I lived with my big cousin Kim and my Auntie Marylyn. She was only in high school taking care of me, feed me, put clothes on me and drive me to different places. She would let me go to her boyfriend’s basketball practice, who later became a professional NBA player. I use to also reminisce about living with my cousin/uncle who was always keeping my hair cut and teaching me how to fight. In this house I also thought about the time my mom and my dad came to my cousin/uncle house past midnight trying to take me with them. I played it back in my mind of how my dad pulled a gun on my cousin/uncle to take me with them. My cousin/uncle still didn’t give in and kept me by his side. I know a lot of you are wondering why I keep writing cousin/uncle, well it’s because he’s actually my aunties son, but he raised me as if he was my uncle.

A lot of African Americans have this in their lives, not sure if it’s just our culture but all over the world it is like this, but after reminiscing about all of all these things I called my grandmother and told her I wanted to move back with Granny and Emmett. As an adult, I understand it was a lot of legal issues and paper work that was involved but at the time I just wanted to change my current situation. After she got better, she made it happen. I was back with my granny and grandfather and was very excited. My granny is very religious and always kept me in the church. Going to church was a lifestyle due to her father being a Pastor. He pastored a small church in Berkeley California called “Bible Way Church”. This was the beginning of one of my talents being birth. When going to church I use to either fall asleep on my granny shoulder or just stare of dude playing the drum set. I started to go home and beat on everything I came in contact with. My granny put pots and pans on the floor and I would beat them with forks and spoons for hours.

After seeing my passion, my granny and Emmett purchased me a drum set which I played each and every day. After my granny’s father passed, I suddenly lost a passion and stop playing the drums. I believe this was the first lost that I encountered in my life. If affected my granny which affected me. Once I stop playing the drums for that period of time, I went back into reminiscing mode. I would visualize times of being with my dad. I remember actually urinating in his bed and him cleaning me off, while us watching batman and robin. I didn’t get into trouble like I did before with my grandmother. I also remembered riding with my dad, my mom and my auntie, and the backdoor opened up on me. I almost fell out the car but thanks to my auntie for grabbing me as hard as she could and closing my door. All these thoughts were running rapid, but made me want a better connection with my dad. I use to go over to my cousins house and they would tell me that they saw my dad, but I never would see him. My mom would state that he was coming to see me, but he never showed up.

"Miracle Baby"

One day I was downstairs of my house playing "Sonic" on the Sega genesis. My granny hollered "D COME UP STAIRS", I thought by the sound of her voice that I was in trouble. When I got upstairs my granny said "D your dad had a heart attack", I said is he ok? She said "NO he passed away". At that moment I couldn't cry, I couldn't be sad, I was kind of numb. I don't know if it was because of our relationship, or because I hadn't seen him in such a long time but I was like "OH DANG". My granny was a very supportive, even though she had never met him, her and Emmett took me to his funeral. Before the funeral though my mom would go to the mortuary and just sit for hours by his casket. She would cry and talk to him as if he could hear her. When she told, I thought it was pretty creepy. But hey "whatever" works for her. She didn't like funerals, so she didn't go to his funeral so I believe that was her spending her last moments with him. When walking into the funeral, it was a bit awkward because not only did he not have obituaries with his face on it, but I didn't know anyone in there. A few ladies said they remembered me and that I looked just like my mom, but I didn't recognize them from Adam or Eve. When the funeral was over, I did remember an older light skin lady with grey long hair. It was my grandmother, who was my dad's mom. She was pure Indian with thick grey hair, standing about 4 foot 5. I hugged her and reminded her of myself. I could sense that she didn't remember me but she was a bit older and walked slouched over. She was a sweet lady.

After reintroducing myself, as I was walking outside, a young lady approached me and asked me if my name was "Darrell". Well I'm use to people calling me "Double D", so I was kind of shocked of how she knew my name. I said yea that's my name and she then hugged me and squeezed me very tight. She said "I AM YOUR SISTER, pops always talked about you, and I remember you from when I was little". She had a little boy standing with her who told me that his name was "Scooter". She was like Scooter, this is your uncle Darrell and you are both the same age. My granny, grandfather, sister and her boyfriend introduced themselves and exchanged umbers. Although it was a crazy event to be meeting, everything happens for a reason.

"Sega is not just a Game"

I mentioned my Sega Genesis earlier, well this system was very significant in my thought process. Although I wasn't super blown by the video game itself, I realized this was a gateway to a lot of things. My granny had a best friend who would bring her granddaughter over to play the Sega genesis with me. This girl was about 7 years older than me, so she was super advanced and I'm not just talking about the video game. She would come over to my house and play the game and insist on doing other things. The naïve me was very uncertain, but the curiosity in me wanted to try it. She would take off her shirt and tell me to "suck on her titties". I wasn't a sucka, so shit, I would suck the shit out of them titties. Now the first time, I was afraid but after years of this, I became a professional titty sucker. I remember one time she pulled down my pants and started to give me falatio. Honestly, this started at the age of 7 and I kind of looked forward to always play the Sega genesis with her. We began to do all the things that grown-ups were doing so I began to become advanced at a young age. All the cousins would come over and play Sega genesis with

"Miracle Baby"

her. We would build tents and have turns playing Sega. At the time I didn't see a problem, well I know this was something I couldn't tell my granny or any other adult, but I also became the man in a sense. I began to go to school and fantasize about the girls in my class and wonder if they were as good as she was on the Sega genesis. This is when I realized this became an addiction of mine that would follow me for the rest of my life.

Growing up I played Babe Ruth baseball for a team called Duvenay. I went to practice one day and was doing catching drills. I was catching every ball that came my way but my coach kept screaming at me saying catch the ball like this. After 5 times of hearing him scream, I said fuck this and fuck you, and walked off the field. My granny was sitting in her yellow Cadillac reading her bible and she asked me what happened? I said granny "I don't want to play baseball no more". She said don't be a quitter Baby. I told her, "Granny I'll rather go to the NBA anyway", she said "What Boy"? Yes granny I'll rather play basketball over baseball any day. My baseball coach would always tell me that I would be a good basketball player, because I use to hoop on the outside courts with my cleats on. They use to always say it was bad to be on concrete with my cleats but I would bring a basketball and my baseball glove to baseball practice and shoot around before and after practice. The day that I walked off the field was the last day was the last day I would wear a baseball uniform. Well, at least that's what I thought. I actually end up playing baseball my senior year in high school, but couldn't make any games due to being in a program called ILSP (Independent Living Skills Program) for foster youth.

"Basketball forever lives on"

Fourth grade is when I actually was blessed to learn the logistics of basketball. One of my best friends and Jumbo Brothers, brought me to one of his basketball practices at Rainbow Recreational center in Oakland California. He told me that I was a 1 which is a point guard. I questioned him about it because I didn't know what the hell that was. He told me to just watch him. Jeremee was only in the fourth grade but played basketball at an 8th grade level. He was just gifted. Jerm could dribble, shoot, pass, rebound, call plays and make his team better. Every day at school, I would play him in hoop to get better. I wanted to dribble like him, I mean this dude had the best handles that I had ever seen, no lie. He could throw the ball behind his back, put the ball under his legs, and change directions all in one motion. I mean he was probably one of the best basketball players in the city for the 4th and 5th graders. We started this brotherhood by the name of Jumbo Brothers founded by Auntie Gale Austin. (RIP) We would recite poems for oratorical contests and win every year. We was able to perform for the channel 2 news. We met the mayor, senator and governor of California. It was very powerful for us young black kids. We stood on the stage in tuxedos and recited these poems that would give people life. This would form a brotherhood forever, me and the guys still keep in contact and show love. RIP Tyrone, Xavier and Deontea.

“Miracle Baby”

“Alamedian Huh???”

Starting 6th grade was very hard for me. I left my brothers who was all going to schools in Oakland. I had to go to school in Alameda California, due to the decisions of my granny and Emmett. I was hella mad at first so I started Chipman Middle School with a chip on my shoulder. I was in Alameda claiming Oakland all day every day. I had to make my presence known. I started fighting to prove my hood which was 55th and let people know that I wasn’t a sucka. Every morning Emmett would walk me to the bus stop after granny said a prayer with me. Once I got on that bus, they know me, they knew that I would clown, be loud, sing songs, rap and crack on people. Each and every bus was tagged with my greatness stating “Double D 5500 HeadBussa”. I remember one particular day, I was on the bus and I screamed out of the window to A OG “Fuck You”. The bus was picking up people from the bus stop and that dude ran on the bus like “What the fuck you say Lil Nigga” I’m thinking like shit I need to get out the back door or it’s my ass. Some older guy stood uo and stopped the OG from approaching me and said “ That’s a young ass kid, get your ass off the bus”. The OG pointed at me and said “ Imma kick your ass” and walked off the bus. I thanked that man for saving me from a ass whooping. All my comrades were laughing and clowning me, but shit, that didn’t stop me from talking more shit.

The good thing that I got out of going to school in Alameda was meeting my music teacher. I was in his music class playing the snare drum. One day after class, I asked him if I could play the drum set. It took me a whole two weeks to actually be brave enough to ask him . He said “yes but only for about 10 minutes”. I got on the drums and never got off. From that day forward, he would let me play he set during class while everyone else was still playing the snare drum. I ended up being the youngest in his jazz band at the middle school. I would have to wake up at 5:30am every morning in order to make jazz band which was right before school started. After school I had basketball practice. So as a young kid I have always had a busy schedule. This explains me as an adult today, very busy. I was honored to meet Ms. Sheila E and Mr. Carlos Santana, due to my music teacher Mr. Yamasaki taking me to one of his gigs as he would call it. He was a great guitarist but an all-around musician. We had holiday band concerts every year. Emmett would video tape them but I have no idea where they are today, but anyway. I would play for my 6th grade band an then turn around and play for the advanced jazz bamd. One year we had 3 drummers, we would switch off. They were both older than me, but could play a little bit. One of the drummers was a black kid and the other was Chinese. Yea they could play but just not better than me. The Chinese boy would always try to throw slick comments at me because I was younger than him. He even threatened to beat my ass when I tried to teach him a fill drum roll for a certain song. Anyway, we was at the band concert and it was time for him to play the drums. He was nowhere to be found, so my teacher insisted on me to play instead. In the middle of me playing, the Chinese drummer

"Miracle Baby"

comes from the back stage area, with a black eye, his lips busted and his shirt half way ripped off. At first he told everyone that he fell off of his bike, but from the damage of his face, I knew that was clearly a lie. When I asked him more than normal, he finally came out and said some dudes had jumped him. I was devastated, I didn't know why that had happened to him. They took his money, jewelry, and his bike and then beat him up. I thought to myself "this guy is hella bold for coming in like this". From that day we formed a friendship, primarily because I was sympathetic about his situation.

7th grade, my granny was still praying with me, and Emmett would still be walking me and my niece to the bus stop. Sometimes we would be waiting for the bus with our neighbor Mr. Felton who was blind. He would always tell me that "It's sad that a lot of people that could see, still don't have a vision". As a kid I didn't quite understand that quote but as an adult I know that Mr. Felton was so right. When I got to alameda, after jazz practice, I would go over to the BV's a famous apartment complex in Alameda to my girlfriend's house. She was a girl that I had met in the 6th grade and ended up feeling real hard. We would always have morning sex, on the living room couch, in her room, or in her mommas room. Her little sister walked in on us a couple times but we would act like we was sleep and then get back to it when she left the room. I remember this one day, she wanted to do it in her mommas bed. I was hella hesitant and skeptical about it but shit I am spontaneous so why not. I'm like cool let's do it, what's the worst that can happen? I'm hitting it missionary style, and I feel my dick and its extra stupid wet. When I pulled out, It's blood on my dick. I was like "What The Fuck". She told me that I had brought her period down and I was hella mad. My shirt was full of blood, so I had to go and cop a whote tee for the $5 from the liquor store. From 7th through 8th grade this would be a ritual. We would have morning sex, well when she was on her period I was just getting head. Man after school we would sometimes go to McDonalds and do it in the bathroom.Till this day people see me and still ask me if I remember that. "I'm like duh dummy it was me. It got so bad that we would have sex at porta potties at the park. After basketball practice we getting it in, before jazz band, we was getting it in. We got it in Monday through Saturday. I don't know if it was love or if it was lust, but we got it in.

After graduating from the 8th grade, I started to go to school on the Alameda Base, and she went to Encinal High School.I thought we would pick up where we left off, really after her spending time all summer at my house and with my family. But no, things became different. I would try to call her, she wouldn't answer. I would go by her school and couldn't find her, and go to her house and she wasn't there. One day I left school early and something told me to go to her house. My cousin and I met up, which was very common, like every day, but went to her house this particular day. I go and knock on the door and I hear talking behind the door. I knocked again and a Mexican dude walk out of the door, with her walking behind him. I asked her "what is this about"? she said "we are not together, why you tripping"? I said "what you mean"? And then she told me to leave her house. I walked out the door in anger and in rage. As I walked pass the glass with the fire extinguisher sitting in it. I punched it with so much force, when I pulled my fist out, my knuckles were cut up and I could see the white meat. The blood was pouring down my hand. My cousin was like "What the fuck" and asked her for a big towel. I told her I was done and we bounced back to Oakland.

9th grade becam harder for me to focus. I was fighting every day like Floyd Mayweather. I would get on the bus by feet and leave school on a bike or a scooter. I had no respect for no one or their things. I remember arguing with my teacher and she said "Darrell you are going to die and you won't be anything in life". I was in shock that she would say that so I said "Fuck You" and left. Eventually I got a letter in the mail stating that school would make me voluntarily leave before getting kicked out of the whole Alameda District. I made the decision to leave and start at Encinal with my cheating ass ex-girlfriend. That summer going into my 10th grade, I was already talking to my friend for about a year but I started to actually feel her as a girlfriend. She was so innocent and very quiet. I couldn't tell her things that I was doing, I didn't want her to know that I was a bad boy. We would talk on the phone from 8 oclock until 1 am in the morning every night. Crazy thing is we was doing this 2 years prior but fell off for some reason. She began to win my heart, but I was in a dilemma with another girl from church. 10th grade I was claiming HB Head Bussa 5500 like no other, stealing cars, and robbing people. At first me and my cousins would wait until my granny went to sleep, and go out the bottom of the house and take her van and joy ride the streets of Oakland. My granny daughter who I call my sister caught us and told granny on us. I confessed and told her that we had a universal key to take her car. I was on punishment for a couple of weeks. We would go to the malls, Bayfair, Southland, Hilltop and others to scissor handily steal cars. We would specifically take Toyotas because they was so easy. One day we was standing outside in the Bayfair Mall parking lot plotting. A lady and her daughter came to her car and put a bag in the trunck, and walked back into the mall. Once we seen the mall door closed, we went to work. We hopped in the car and drove straight to the town (Oakland). My cousin would later get caught in the car for driving it to school. He went to juvenile hall with the police pointing guns at him.

"Couldn't get Away"

When school started, I was juggling two girlfriends but still playing drums, basketball and rapping. I played for the JV team as a freshmen but was later moved to varsity. I played my heart out against them upperclassmen. They tried to beat me up on the court to prove that I wasn't going to take their spot. I went to every practice. I even practiced when I was sick with the flu to show my dedication to the team. I remember one day my cousin and a couple of our goons came to the football game. My cousin was walking in with gloves on as I was about to leave with my teammate from basketball practice. I already knew what that meant, either they were in a stolo (Stolen car) or they was about to get on somebody head (Rob someone), shit, knowing them it probably was both. That night my cousin told me that we had a car and it was parked on 55th. That morning I left out to go to summer practice as I normally would. I walked to go and get the car to drive to practice. As I opened the door, I looked ahead at the corner and noticed the damn Oakland Police Department car. I instantly got out the car and closed the door. I ran so fast up the hill with my gym bag attached to my shoulder and knocking against my leg. As I was running, I seen a house door open. All I thought was "Thank You God". I ran into the house in fear and in a panic. A Caucasian lady said "What are you doing in here"? She seemed to be very scared and in shock. I told her that a dog was chasing me and that I was scared. She walked outside and saw the police, she flagged them down and told them that I had just ran into her house. The police said "Son I seen you run from that car" Why did you run? "Are you old enough to even drive" As he finished that last question I shitted on myself LOL… Naw I'm joking, but I told them that it was my mom's idea. It was one African American lady police with an African American male police. I was so scared, my dreads was in my face and I was just flowing with sweat. I told myself that if I got out of that situation I would cut my dreads immediately. They put me in the hand cuffs and ran my information. After that, they talk to me about my actions, but I wasn't listening due to me being so scared shitless. They called my granny. When they called my granny I was like "Oh Shit" in my mind. I didn't say it, but in my mind I did. Luckily my house was right up the hill from where I was or I would have been going to juvenile hall. When my granny came, I told her that my mom told me to go and get this car and bring it to her. She said that she knew what I was doing and begin to whoop my ass with her slide on shoes. I'm sitting in the back seat of the police car, still cuffed as she was whooping my face, my legs, and my chest. Smacked in the face a couple of times but I was just happy that I wasn't going to juvenile Hall. The police took the cuffs off of me and allowed me to go on with my granny.

When I got off of punishment I headed back into the streets. I would go to 76 and Nay street where my sister lived to link up with the HB's. (Head Bussas). We would slap box in the middle of the street, steal cars, rob people, fight and get on chicks. One night, it was a party across the street from our bricks where we hung. We see hella chicks walking into that thang, so you know we had to be apart. Once it got dark, we gathered about 8 of us and walked over to the party. While we was there, some S.T.I.G (Scandalous type individual girls) which was a gang was like "Here go them bitch ass HB niggas" My big cousin "G" who was fearless and drunk, raised his hand and smack the shit out of her. We grabbed him out of the party and left the party. When we got down the street, a big ass truck pulled up on us. Some dude in the truck lowered his window and said "You niggas don't want it". I yelled out "Fuck you suckas" and that's when it went down. These niggas hopped out of 2 trucks with about 12 niggas. Here we was squobbing (Fighting) in the middle of the street. It was a big ass brawl. I'm punching niggas left and right. My cousin had two niggas on him, when I went to pull one of them niggas off of him, my lil nigga shot his gun in the air. Everybody scattered, then jumped back into the trucks and left. My cousin was leaking blood from his lip but was laughing as if this wasn't shit. This is the day HB became truly official. 3 days later, some niggas start shooting at us, as we ran into one of our affiliate's house. Niggas was hot, so we all started to be strapped up with guns.

"Losing aint easy"

Summer is over and back to school I had to go. I was pulled from Varsity back to the JV team due to a couple of practices I missed from being out thugging. One morning after getting on 3 buses to get to school, I seen one of them suckas that we had a big ass brawl with. I had my gun on me so the first thing I thought to do was to shoot. I start shooting in the air and he took off running. Yea I was a hot head, I was the dude in the party with the gun in the air dancing with chicks. Anyway, I put my gun in my back pack and went to school like nothing happened. The next morning I got on the bus, my cuz Jerm got on the same bus. He would get on the bus periodically with me because he start going to Alameda High School. He was playing basketball but had just joined the same gang we was rivaling with, STI . I told him what had happened the night of the brawl, but he finished my sentences as if he already knew. The word got around fast and the funk was real between everybody. When talking to him, I asked him about this nigga that I seen him with hella times before. I told Jerm "I use to go to school with dude and I don't trust him". Jerm was like " Oh that's my STI Nigga, he a real nigga". I told him about my guns and we laughed and joked. Actually that week Jerm used my dress shoes for some Hoop Banquet for some basketball team. That nigga always did know how to finesse" LOL. The next week I was looking for Jerm on the bus but he didn't get on. I asked his teammate about him and he said "that nigga been catting off and not coming to school". By the way, Catting off means "faking, not being serious, or not showing up". I knew how life had got with us thugging, but didn't know the extent of how he was going about it. The next week was very tragic, I remember it like it was yesterday. When I got to school, my lil sister T asked me if I had looked at the news, I said "Real Niggas don't look at the News". She was like well ST Jacari got killed. I didn't know him but I did remember Jerm bringing him up in certain conversations. I asked her to get me a newspaper from the office. When I read it, the article said it could possibly be someone else and not Jacari. A upper class man came up to me and said " Blood I'm sorry about your cousin". I'm like which cousin you talking about? He then said "Jerm bruh. I said "that wasn't Jerm, that was Jacari who got smacked". He said "Na bruh Jerm had Jacari ID in his pocket". My lil sis T had come up and gave me a hug as if she already knew the real story. I instantly start punching the walls and kicking shit. The upperclassman knew me as an young real nigg,a so they gave me the respect as such. I told them to give me a ride to Jem house, which was in Oakland. I left school before 1st period started. When I got to his house everybody was crying and in shock. The nigga that I asked Jerm about a week prior, was the same nigga who shot my cousin in his back and killed him. The death of my cousin made mr realize how short life was.

"Change is Good"

It was hella hard for me to get over the death of Jerm. I tried to keep myself productive without doing dumb shit. I started making shirts with his face on them. The Jumbo Brothers did a tribute to Jerm at his funeral, and we all broke down after performing from the front of the church. After his funeral, I got my first tattoo to honor him, which is a man doing the east bay funk (A famous dunk) on my left arm. I was in a state of depression for about 3 months. It fucked with me not only because my cuz was just killed, but because I knew I could be next if I didn't change. I was robbing, stealing, shooting, getting shot at, and living ruthless, but yet I was still alive. I made a plan to change my life around. I was in a bad mood so I snapped on everybody. One day during 6th period, my ex got into my face talking some dumb shit. She said that her boyfriend was going to whoop my ass. When the bell rung, I walked across the street where he was and said "Whats Up". Mind you, it was the same dude that walked out of her house with her when I punched that glass. He said "I heard you wanted to fight me nigga". I was like "Nah bruh" and stuck my hand out to act as if I was giving him a hand shake. As he was about to shake my hand I fired on him. BOOM!!!! I start whooping his ass and he dropped to the ground. He was about 2 years older than me and here I was whooping the dog shit out of him. The police let off their sirens and as I looked up at them, he stuck me dead in my jaw. Spectators start asking him if he was ok due to me whooping his ass. The police cuffed him because he was considered trespassing from coming to my school and damn near being an adult. I was forced to go to the office and call my granny. She wasn't mad but understood that it might be my last chance at attending that school. I was suspended and then expelled from Encinal High School. They gave me until the next school year to leave so I finished out the year there, Thank GOD. I was tired of being rejected and always subject to be in trouble. I made up my mind to make shirts, play basketball and do music.

"Unc Saved Us"

I start training for basketball that summer and ended up getting a starting position on John C Fremont high school basketball team. At Fremont, I was able to start fresh. I wasn't stealing cars no more, had a couple of robberies, but for the most part I start seeing change in myself. One day after basketball game, my past life would revisit and make me revert back to my old ways. My cousin came up to me and

“Miracle Baby”

said that some niggas kept pointing at me and my other little cousin, while we was on the court playing. We were actually facing Damien Lillard and his high school team Oakland High. My cousin overheard those niggas talking about a shootout or something. So apparently my cousin and his friends had previously shot at these dudes at a party. I didn’t know and had nothing to do with it. After the game as I’m driving out the parking lot of Fremont by the basketball gym with my two cousins. A nigga start putting his crutch up to my window almost hitting me in the face. He was cripple and all I thought was I’m about to run this nigga over. My cousin yelled “Don’t go straight Nigga” but me being hard headed, I hit the gas almost hitting him. As we pulled out the drive way I see a big ass van in the middle of the street. Some fat dude hopped out the van and start shooting. We was in the middle of the cross fire as they were shooting at each other but we was very blessed. That night we strapped up and went looking for them niggas but they was nowhere to be found. Years later, the same apartments that we were searching for them niggas at, my daughter end up being raised in. After the chaos, I hollered at my uncle/cousin who was from the same hood as them niggaz. He set up a “Peace meeting”. He called me and my cousins to come and squash the beef. We went to their hood to show respect. As me and my bruhcuz walked up to the car, my little cousin stayed in the car. These niggas sitting side by side on the trunk of a buick with a AR-15 and a .357 laying on their laps. My Uncle told them that we was Hooper’s and wasn’t about that life. My big cousin Henry walked up from out of nowhere. One of them was like “ A blood you gotta cut”, my cousin said “Its good”, but I knew he was strapped and plotting, because I had actually left my gun in the car with my little cousin. After Unc said what he said, we all shook hands and made peace.

After this incident I prayed long and hard to God about changing my ways. He had saved me so many times and I owed it to him to show my appreciation. I start rapping gospel with my cousin and formed a group. We was called the “Gospel Gorillas” and would perform at many churches and community events. We won a number of talent shows and became recognized by many people in our city. My cousin begin to venture off and make other music and became successful so shortly after I began to express myself in other ways as well. I never left gospel, but I knew that in order to reach a certain population, I couldn’t be placed in one category. Some of our songs are still played and recognized such as “Gospel Gorilla” and “Keeping It Real”. As I spoke in previous chapters before, I was still juggling girlfriends but was trying to keep it under control. I had a freshman at my school, a girl at my church, a girl in Vallejo who had been rocking with me for many years and a junior at my school who was working a job and looking out for me. I would go to school with about $20 dollars in my pocket and leave with about $100-$150 dollars. OH YEA I had 2 other girls but only 1 or 2 had my heart no lie. The summer of my Junior year I was blessed to participate in the summer bridge enrichment program at Cal Maritime College, due to my good grades and my achievements. I was referred by my academic counselor who always looked out for me. I was a great teacher's pet my junior year. I use to buy my teacher lunch of course with her money and I would get free lunch. My attitude changed tremendously and I was still rocking my 19 gold teeth. Anyway, at this program I would have multiple girls come and visit me. They would bring me food, money and even sex lol. During this program, I realized the wrong that I was doing with juggling all these girls and their hearts. I had to make a decision to change and start cutting chicks off one by one. When school started back, I was more focus and applying to colleges. Growing up my granny would always tell me that I was going to college. I grew up saying that I was going to attend Morehouse College and become a Morehouse Man. Before I graduated high school I was blessed to go on a Historically Black College tour. We went to so many colleges, I can't remember all of them. We visited South Carolina A&T, Howard University, Clark Atlanta, Morehouse, Hampton and a few more. When we got to Morehouse, you know I had to cop me a hoody. Everybody that know me, know that I am very big on fashion. Morehouse is connected to Clark Atlanta and Spellman. Spellman is a college full of women and I was so juiced to know that. Due to Dr. Martin Luther King graduating from Morehouse, and my granny always pushing me to attend, I made up in my mind that I was at my future College. When we got there and did the tour, I noticed there were no ladies walking around the campus. They said one thing that completely turned me off was that the college was an all men's college, and we were not able to bring ladies to the campus. I instantly reconsidered my decision. After all these years my granny instilled Morehouse College in me, she never once told me about it being an all men's college.

"Don't Kiss No ASS"

On that college tour I was able to meet some good people. One of my friends that I met on this tour went on to be one of the best song writers of our generation, and sell a lot of records. He has a lot of clot within the music industry, but have once to make a song with me. Thinking about it, we were more close when we were broke. When he got a little recognition he moved from the hood that grew up on and became "Hollywood" literally. I'm not saying bruh had to help me with my career but I saved him many times in the hood from getting robbed, shot, or even killed. We came from the same humble beginnings, so I thought it would be quite different. I use to take bruh to his shows only to show support and it was times I had to check niggas from getting at him. He a lil nigga so, everybody tried to test him but me baing who I am that wasn't going to happen. I always been the dude to congradulate my people on their success, but I also was taught to never forget where I come from. Our friendship is not mutual and I don't kiss ass, I wish him the best with his career, but shit life goes on. I call, no answer, I text, no text back so Good luck Bruhcuz. 5500 all day everyday. If yall ever here my name Double D in a song just know who bruh is talking about.

After the college tour, It was back to the ghetto I went. In order to stay out the hood, I stayed in the gym or inside of the studio. Everyday after school, I would go to the boys and girls club to hoop with my niggas. Me and my potnas would run games for hours and hours. One of my lil niggas end up playing for the Warriors D League and then overseas. Me and my boy Ron, who was also on my high school basketball team would go head to head everyday. Somedays we would do nothing but shoot all 3s and somedays we would do drills. Ofcourse I use to always win, but Ron had game as well. He was going through similar situations that I was facing with his mom. We had these things in common such as our moms suffering from drug addiction along with the basketball skills that we shared. Ron and I became hella close on and off the court. One day after school, I went to the boys and girls club as I usually do, but this day seemed really weird. No one was in the gym and it just felt empty. Later that night when I got home, I got a call from one of my teammates. He was like "Double D!!!" I'm like "Whats Good" he said " Bruh, Ron was at the club and niggas start fighting, I'm like yea so did he whoop dude? He said "Naw bruh he wasn't even fighting" I'm like OK nigga what happened then? He said "Bruh they start shooting and Ron got hit". Instantly, I dropped the phone.I didn't want to g=hear the rest of the story but I kind of got the gist of that call. My boy Ron was sitting in the car, waiting for our homeboy who we use to hoop with. He was hollering at a chick and then a fight broke out. Somebody start shooting and Ron got hit in his head by a stray bullet and died on the spot. Just when things start going up for me, I got hit with some more shit again. I didn't want to go to school, I didn't even want to play hoop but I couldn't quit neither. To cope with things like this, I always would escape with having sex and drinking. I start wilding again, and had no remorse for what I was doing. The girl that had rocked with me ever since I was 14. She was my girlfriend and my prom date although I went to about 5 proms. When I was with her, it was about her, but when I left, it was like out of sight out of mind. I was taking girls virginity left and right, really start feeling numb to it. I would use condoms but still was mistreating my body.

"The Abortion"

After being presented with "Prom King" I was focused on going to college but still distracted by the ladies. I remember one day, one of the girls I was talking to came to my school with a shirt on that read "Double D's World". I felt like the man on campus but I didn't understand how deep it would get. We was kicking it but it wasn't that serious to me. This is the same one I spoke about earlier who looked out for me. She cashed out on my speakers for my car, my gold teeth, clothes, shoes, and of course food. One day she called me while I was just getting out of ILSP program. She stated that she was pregnant but didn't think she would be keeping it. I told her that if she needed some money for the procedure I would gladly help her. She said she had it and that she thanked me for wanting to help her out. About a month past, I'm with the squad in purple ville apartments in San Leandro California, where my cousins was selling marijuana at. I start feeling hella sick and threw up. We went to get some ginger ale from the store, and I threw up in the store. We spent the night in purple ville because I was in no condition to drive. We were messing with chicks out there anyway but still. The next day, I get a call from the chick, and these niggaz was hella loud in the back ground, so I had to walk out of the apartment. She said "Double D, I went and got it done today. I said "What? What are you talking about?" she said, "The abortion". I was kind of sad for her but felt relieved. She was crying and gave me the rundown of the procedure of the whole abortion. When we got off the phone, I instantly ran in the house and told all my cousins what she said. I was juiced because that shit had my mind and body all fucked up.

In the mist of all of that, I was still hooping, rapping, playing the drums, and creating shirts. From the hard I work of my junior and senior year, I ended up with the highest G.P.A at Paul Robeson Preparatory College at Fremont High. I got accepted to so many colleges but had to make a smart decision of where to go. Oh, I forgot to tell yall, when my granny decided to move to Ohio my junior year, the first week of my senior year was spent at Trotwood High School in Trotwood Ohio. I attended Trotwood High for only a week because of the testing that I already passed in Oakland along with my basketball team. I told my granny that I rather go back to Oakland and finish up. I moved in with my grandmother who welcomed me with open arms. 3 months before graduating high school, I decided to commit to Central State University in Wilberforce Ohio. In the window of our school office, they had pictures of the graduating seniors displayed with the colleges that accepted us. Under my picture it was about 10 colleges that accepted me and believe it or not some schools even wanted me for basketball. I felt like finally my life was getting back on track. My mom was in a drug rehabilitation program, I was playing drums for 2 churches, and some schools wanted me to hoop for them. When I graduated high school, all of my family attended. My granny even hopped on the plane from Ohio to see me walk the stage.

"Princess"

I had accomplished something in my life that was really important to my family. I felt on top of the world and no one could have taken me down. After graduation,

"Miracle Baby"

our class president threw a graduation party on 55th. When I got out of my car to walk inside, a little white Chihuahua walked up to me wagging its tail. The little dog was so adorable. As hood as I was, I couldn't let the dog stray away. I picked the dog up, found one of my class mates boxes, and put the dog in it, in the back seat of my car. I walked into the party feeling like I just saved the World. That night the dog came with me to my house and I cared it as if it was a baby. I called my granny who had come back to visit me for my graduation, and told her about me finding the dog, well in reality the dog had found me. At first she was very hesitant about accepting me keeping it, but once she saw the tiny little dog, she couldn't resist it either. After a week of that dog living in a box and going everywhere I went, my granny got the dog shots, bought her a cage and everything that comes along with it. After giving her the proper treatment, my granny then flew her and the dog to Ohio. She said "D, you don't even have a name for her". I said "granny, I'm a king and you are already treating her like royalty, so name her Princess". Princess became a part of the family and everybody treated her as such.

Before leaving Oakland, my granny gave me $1000 dollars, I was going to throw an going away party with it. The party didn't happen due to the age limit and a few other minor problems, so I end up going to Ohio and buying some rims for the Buick that we had shipped out there. My grandfather (Emmett) was with me every step of the way when I got the rims. My granny thought it was real stupid of me to spend $1000 dollars on rims but it was something that I wanted. I just had graduated high school, I had a Buick on dubs and I was out of my city and state, couldn't tell me I wasn't winning. When I touched down in Ohio, I met my cousins who were my age. They was hella funny and goofy like me but I can't lie, it was hard as hell leaving everybody in Oakland. I cried when I thought about it, but I wanted something new. My girl at the time from the church. Had come to help me unpack and move into the dorms at my college. She came all the way to Ohio from Oakland to help me, now that's love. Man the experience was very refreshed. Walking on the College campus was like a dream come true. The Marching band was marching in the middle of the street playing the tone "I'm so glad I go to CSU". Of course I didn't know that song as a freshman just coming in, but later I eventually found out. I got situated inside of the school, it was so many beautiful women just walking past me, some were friendly and some weren't. I felt like I was in Heaven though. I left the ghetto and went to a college campus. I start calling all my cousins like "Nigga, I'm in College, and it's some fine ass chicks in this thang". I remember in orientation I met this girl who was cute from Detroit Michigan (The D), she seemed down to earth and always cracking jokes, just in the meantime of us talking. When school came in session, long story short she became my girlfriend. Anyway, Ione night I'm lying in the dorm room just chilling, mind you Ohio is 3 hours different from California. So it's about 10pm in Ohio and 7pm in California. I get a call from this chick, yea the one who had the abortion about 5 months ago, well at least that's what she told me. We are talking briefly, at the time she is at Grambling University and I'm at Central State University. We chop it up for a min about school and how things were going, but I had class in the morning so I told her that I would hit her phone later.

"Aw Hell Naw" Hell Yea!!!

For 2 days she called me and we would talk about random shit. So the next day when she called me I said, "What's up why all of a sudden you hitting me up"? She say "Double D, I have something to tell you" I'm like what's good? She said "I'm 5 months pregnant, and I'm going to have your baby". I instantly go off on her like "I thought you had an abortion"? Didn't you give me the run-down of you having a fucking abortion? So you telling me you lied? Why are you trying to trap me? She start crying as I'm questioning her and stated that she was sorry for lying to me. I was so pissed said "Bitch you trying to trap me huh"? "I can't believe you fucking lied to me". Here I was just adapting to College as a freshman, and getting hit with a big ass responsibility. Four months later, I was on the speaker phone with her best friend while she was giving birth to my daughter Zaniya Je'Vais Smith. March 8th 2007 to be exact.

"Grind Alone"

It wasn't until 3 months later until I got to physically hold my baby. She was a happy baby, real little but very observant. Here I was a freshman in college at the age of 19 years old and a Dad. The first time holding her, I was so nervous due to her being so tiny and fragile, but it was definitely something I can get used to. It was another summer and I couldn't be broke with a new born, so I start washing cars with my

“Miracle Baby”

daughter’s granddad and her uncle and I start selling weed on the side. My auntie and cousins use to have little buds from a plant, which I would bag up and sell. I kept a back pack full of weed and money. I was mobbing in a rental truck from a cars salesman, who was repairing my car that I was purchasing from him. I would be from 55th in East Oakland all the way to Vallejo if I had to, grinding real hard. Me and my 2 nephews start linking up to hit the studio and make music, long story short, my backpack came up missing with at least $1500 dollars and $500 dollars’ worth of tree (marijuana). I was pissed and unsure of where my back pack had went. I don’t judge or point the blame due to me being very loyal, but I learned that day that’s it better to grind alone.

One night me and my cousins were about to go to a house party, It was me and about 7 of them. I remember like it was yesterday, I had this black and gold ecko jacket on with my black and gold J’s (Jordans) with a mouth full of gold grill in my mouth. We was outside just pregaming before the party, drinking and some people were smoking. We see a couple of chicks across that street that looked descent, not hella fine, but not ugly either. My cousin hollered at one of them and told her to come and kick it. My cousins went in the house as I stayed leaning on the car, texting this lil chick. One of the woman came up to me and said “ I want to taste your dick right now” I’m like “Right Now, Right Now” she said “What, you scared”? Knowing me, I wasn’t no pussy, so I whipped out. As soon as I whipped out, she start mopping me, meaning giving me oral sex in the street while leaning on the car. Anybody could see us and she didn’t care I guess neither did I. My little cousin Tooda came from around the corner and all I heard was his ass laughing hella loud. He went inside of the house and told all my cousins, but when they came out side she was done. We finally got into our cars I believe about 3 cars deep to go to that house party. This when our family ran deep, no one left no one behind. I miss the good ol days. When we got there, we seen some cats that my cousin had just recently got into it with. My cousin went up to one of the dudes and exchanged some words. I was a bit across the room getting twerked on by some little chick. I’m watching him as she dances on me. Next thing you know, the music is shut off and a big ass brawl begin. One of them niggas start shooting our way and we start shooting back. Thank God nobody was hit and we all made it home safe, but that was one hell of a day/night.

"Miracle Baby"

Before going back to college, I always cried while holding my daughter close to my chest. Knowing that it would be a while until I could hold her again. It was a crazy feeling not knowing if she would be safe and that I would be missing out on her growing up or possibly speaking her first words. As I boarded the plane I was excited to go back to college but still sad about leaving my baby.

"Sophomore Year"

I started my sophomore year of college very strong. I hit the ground running. Because I got hurt with a serious ankle injury and I couldn't play basketball, I decided to experience something different in my life. I did a lot of researching, a lot of praying to God, and a lot of contemplating on deciding to go the route that most people yearned for in college. I kept seeing around campus how the Black Greek Organizations were the ones giving all the events on campus and giving back to the community while being very educational. I was at a party one night and I kept seeing these cats throwing up "Hang Loose" or in Oakland "Seminary" with their hand gestures. I seen this fraternity on Television before and instantly remember reading a book about Dr. Martin Luther King being a part of this fraternity. I accidently walked through their line in a party and damn near got jumped. I just seen all of them walking together but didn't think anything of it. One of the dudes was like "He a young cat bruhs, stall em out". I was thinking dude damn near saved me from an ass whooping but I wasn't about to show no fear.I told bruh my bad and good looking out for me.

As I was leaving out one of my classes in Banneker Hall, I seen a flier on the wall stating about an informational. It was the same fraternity that I had just almost got jumped by. I went to the library and considered the fraternity more. I felt confident about the frat and decided to try out the informational. When I got into the informational it was hella people sitting in the desk while the Men of Alpha Phi Alpha Fraternity Inc, Delta Xi Chapter were greeting each individual at the door as GDI's walked in. When I walked in, one of them was like "I remember you little nigga" I start laughing and said "Yea, I bet you do my bad". He laughed and I proceeded to find my seat. It seemed like everybody that was either a basketball player, football player, thugs, and sophisticated was sitting in that informational. They had us introduce ourselves briefly and give a back drop of our back ground. When it got to me I said " My name is Darrell Smith, I'm a Business Major and my classification is a sophomore. I'm from Oakland California and I just had a baby girl. Everyone clapped, but when I sat down all I can think of was my daughter and begin to block out everything and everyone around me. The Men of Alpha, gave the history of the fraternity and stated why they had join the fraternity. I was impressed because in the party these dudes reminded me of me and my cousins rocking together in Oakland. In this informational they were all business men handling business. Shortly after that day, It was a party at the Masonic Hall that the Alpha's were having in Xenia, the city about 15 minutes from the college. Me and a couple of my homies got drunk as hell and went to that thang. Girls were twerking, cups were getting passed around, blunts were being lit and the music as popping. That night the DJ even shouted me out and played my song titled "Bounce That Ass". I was impressed by everybody dancing to it too, I can't even front. I was dancing with a chick and one of the Men of Alpha came up to me, whispered in my ear "get me your transcript as soon as possible". When I left the party hella juiced (Happy) not only because they played my song at the party, but one of the members from the fraternity I wanted to join just hollered at me. I went back to school and told my girlfriend at the time. She was happy for me and we celebrated with bottles and sex. I had gotten my transcripts and everything else necessary and gave it to bruh. About two weeks went by and I got a call telling me to meet up. I was given specific instructions of things to bring, where to be at and the exact time to be there. When I got to the destination, it was a bunch of them dudes from the informational standing around, but this time no one was dressed to impress. I had a lime green shirt on, red monkey jeans and some lime green and orange Nike loafers. Boy was I clowned for them bright ass colors. I was roasted for about an hour about my gear. After that day, I already knew what the rest of the school year was going to consist of, long nights and short days.

"Long Nights and Short Days"

When I got to the house of Alpha, I remember walking down some stairs and seeing this one dude that always was talking shit on the basketball court. We almost fought a couple of times and everyone knew us being on the basketball court together would either end in a bunch of threats with profanity or a big ass fight. I wanted to beat his ass every time I seen his little bony ass. When I saw him I thought "This bitch ass nigga in here, AWWW Hell NAWWWW. Going through the process of pledging the hate turn into dislike, and then into love in a matter of months. We had about 22 dudes wanting to join this frat but it would all have to be proven. We worked out together, ate together, and hung out on the yard together. The man who showed us the important of brother hood was MeShawn "Mr. Brown" Brown. He was hella cool and always cracked jokes. He used to always be like "I'm fresh from head to feet with Polo". He stayed in Polo Ralph Lauren like he was sponsored by them. For some reason, he was always on the phone but still helping us with our show. Whenever his phone would ring, his ring tone would go off singing "I got my drink and my 2 step" by Cassidy, an famous rapper from

Philly. We would all bust out with a dance whenever the song would go off. He seemed to be always hanging up or getting hung u on so we stayed hearing "I got my drink and my 2 step" and we would always dance right along with it. After so long, these cats that were dancing and exercising with me became some of my closest friends. We shared so many memories and stories. I remember one day, one of my line brothers was driving our other line brother car. He tried backing up to be close to the ATM machine at the bank for MeShawn and smacked into a divider. MeShawn start rolling, I mean cracking up so hard that it made me laugh. He was like "DAMN" and start rolling LOL. We were mad because this was the only car we had to get around with but MeShawn was just showing us that things happen in life that's out of our control and sometimes you just have to laugh. He didn't make a big deal, he told my line brother not not trip and to keep his head up. I believe it wasn't until after we became Alphas until my line brother told our other line brother about the incident. Another time, we were parking inside of Anderson Hall parking lot and my line brother crazy ass parked the same car on a big ass heel of snow. Why? I do not know, but we spent about an hour and thirty minutes shoveling that car down from that heel of snow. It was about 7 of us out there shoveling. We were taught to be discreet, but that day a lot of people on campus seen us looking very suspicious. Here it is a couple of dudes that never use to hang out on campus are all of a sudden working together, in sweats, hoodies and beat up ass shoes and having fun doing it.

"Decemeber 4th isn't just Founders Day"

December 4th is Alpha Phi Alpha Fraternity Founder's Day meaning that was the day that the fraternity was founded in 1906. The Alphas would always throw a big party and a March for Dr. Martin Luther King every year. I said earlier that it was 22 that started out with us, well only 11 people had dropped off the line. All 11 of us were cleaning and decorating the Masonic Hall for the party. Mind you, I have yet to go to sleep and I had just gotten from work after classes. We were all tired but I knew that I was tired. I was delusional but still was going hard with cleaning and decorating. MeShawn seen me craking jokes and he was like "I see you like to play a lot", I said "Yea man to cover up all my pain". When we were finishing up MeShawn said he needed a ride somewhere and the to his sandz house. My line brother said he was tired and asked me to do him of favor to drive. He handed me the keys and we proceeded to go to the car. Whenevr we left, we left out in groups of 2. "Never leave your brother behind" that's what we were taught. So, my line brother, MeShawn and I rode together. I was driving, MeShawn was in the passenger seat and my line brother was directly behind me. I remember MeShawn saying "Don't nobody fall asleep" I'm like "I'm not". As we got on the highway, I can feel me drifting to the left and I'll open muy eyes. At that point MeShawn

“Miracle Baby”

and my line brother is sleep. I would be driving for about 10 minutes and find myself opening my eyes periodically. I finally got to the destination of the navigation, and tell him “We are here”. He says, “Wait out here and I’ll be back”. He came back like 45 minutes to an hour later, at least that’s what it felt like. I got to dose off and take a quick nap before hopping back on the road. When he got back he asked if I could take him to his sandz house now. I rolled down the window, put back on my seat belt and drove off. We were riding in my line brother’s little ecofriendly Prius. My knees were touching the steering wheel, that’s how small this car was. As I’m driving, I start drifting again. When I feel myself drifting I open my eyes once again. I turned up the music and even rolled down all the windows in the car this time to keep myself awake. I finally get off the high way and unto the street. I remember making an right turn onto the street and passing up a cemetery on my left side and a gas station on my right. As the car is rolling, I here “BAM”. I open my eyes from the pressure and the impact. I ran into a telephone pole and the car was smoking. The airbag had shot into my chest with full force. I look to the right, and said “Mr. Brown” are you ok”? He was like “AWW, AWW” and stayed laid back on the seat. I turned around around and seen my line brother face with blood on it. He said “I can’t move’ so I pulled him from over the seat and placed him gently on the ground . I wiped the blood from his face with my jacket not thinking to utilize my shirt.

At this point, its a lot of people standing outside. I go back to check on MeShawn and ask him if he needed me to help him get out but he did not respond. Suddenly the ambulance come. It was 3 ambulances, my back was in pain along with my chest, I couldn’t believe what had just happened. People were asking me if I was OK but all I can say is that “I fell asleep, I fell asleep” “I can’t believe I fell asleep”. I was in shock and everything was going so fast at this moment. When I got in the ambulance, I called my grandmother and told her what happened, and that I was on the way to the hospital. When I was getting treated after about 20 to 30 mins, I asked the doctor “How is my brother doing? She said “He can’t walk but he’s liable to recover very soon. Then I asked “What about Mr. Brown, how is he? She said “Sorry Darrell, he didn’t make it”. I said “What” she said again “He didn’t make it”, I said NO and started screaming and crying. I couldn’t believe this had just happened. I fell asleep and MeShawn had passed away. As I’m crying my line brother who was also my roommate at the time came to get me. He start crying and then I start crying again. When we walked out of the room, their was a lot of people from school in the lobby. Frats, Sorority members, school board members, basketball, football players, band members and more. I felt very useless, very confused, lost and unsure of why this had happened. When my line brother drove me home which was in Trotwood. I was silent and he was like “ It’s not your fault” but that’s all I could think was it was my fault. When I finally got home, my granny met me outside. When I saw her, I instantly start crying. We start crying together. She hugged me real tight and told me that everything would be OK and that she truly truly loved me. He said she don't know what she would have done if I wasn't there. I questioned her, I questioned myself, I even questioned GOD. When I went to the funeral it was jam packed. Mr. Brown was truly loved. He was well respected and well represented by his community, our college, his friends, family and his fraternity. The Alphas called me after the funeral to come and talk to them on campus. They rode me around the campus and just talk to me. They were telling me that it wasn't my fault and that they were there for me if I needed anything. One of them made a call as they were talking to me. He told whoever he was talking to that he had to take over the arrangements of a certain task due to his brother passing away. They made me feel good to know that they weren't mad at me and that they understand my pain. Shortly after, I was in court fighting a case of vehicular homicide and manslaughter. My granny had hired the most expensive lawyer in Dayton Ohio to plead my case. While I was going over my poems and my steps for our pro show, I was in and out of court fighting this case. I knew God was by my side and he knows my heart. I thank God that I beat that case and I walked out of court as a free man. For our pro show we paid a tribute to Meshawn K-9 Brown. It was very sad but well needed. It was 11 of us and they gave us the name "Thin Ice". On March 28th 2008 we became a part of the best fraternity in the world , Alpha Phi Alpha Fraternity Incorporated Delta Xi Chapter . I wish I could change a lot of things that happened but I'm a firm believer that God doesn't make any mistakes. While I was online my momma girlfriend was killed by the police, my cousin was incarcerated and my big cousin had also passed away.

Family is Forever

When I finished that semester, I went home to join my family and be with my daughter. I took my little cousins out to have dinner I think it was Tooda, Pooka, Nook and Wooda because I was balling with refund checks lol. We were talking about how we use to pan-handle, steal, rob and hustle for money when we was younger. We had a great time. After dropping all my cousins off, I went to be back with my daughter. Like every time before, whenever I would leave her, I would cry like a baby. After spending time with my family, I had to head back to school once again. When I got back to school, one day during my lunch break I received a call from my cousin. He was talking about how some dudes came to the window of the house, with mask on and pointed a gun at my cousin who was in the room. I told him to tell everybody to cut, at least for the week. He told me what happened and why these dudes were there. Apparently, my little cousin robbed a dude for his chain, making him get booty butt naked in front of his chick. The dude of course wanted his chain back, so my cousin sold the chain back to him. A couple of days later, the dude came back. In the house, it was all of my cousins, boys, girls, women and men. My girl cousin saw the dude point the gun inside of the window and start screaming to the top of her lungs, she screamed as loud as she could, out of shock and fear. When she screamed, the dude that was masked, ran away. As my cousin was telling this over the phone, my blood was boiling and I was just angry. All I can say was "Yall niggas need to get the fuck up out of there, before they be on some dumb shit". About a week later, tragedy had struck and they came back on some dumb shit. My cousins were all chilling in the same house as we always did. None of them left from the last incident. They were playing games, listening to music, talking, laughing and eating. My little cousin Tooda was working on his rubic cube as always, while he waited for the joystick on Madden. They hear a knock at the door, nobody moved. Another knock occurred at the door, so my big cousin said "I got it". My little cousin Tooda said " don't trip, I'll get it". When he went to open the door and say who is it? A big BOOM!!! Went through the door. My little cousin Tooda said "I'm hit" and start gasping for air. He laid on his stomach as if he was saying a prayer. My big cousin held him in his arms as he was fighting for his life. My uncle and my cousin ran outside with the guns but whoever it was that had just shot my cousin had got away. On November 11, 2009, my baby cousin Phillip Tooda Wright took his last breath to join his mom up in Heaven. About a year later, my cousin who robbed the guy for his chain, was shot about 19 times as he tried to fled the scene from enemies. He was killed on the spot driving somebody's vehicle. My family was devastated and very over whelmed from all of the deaths that were taking place with the younger generation. Here I was in school and couldn't be there, not even mentally. I begin to start smoking heavy weed as well as drinking. Before lunch I was smoking, after classes I was smoking, before bed I would smoke a blunt, I didn't get enough. My mom would always say "You love your weed huh?" yea kind of. I actually fell in a deep form of depression. I had lost so many people within the matter of months. My grades start lacking and I begin to give up.

"Don't Give UP, New Beginnings Begin"

My girlfriend and I had broken up due to the neglect of both parties but mainly me. I seemed to be getting hit left and right. One day as I was walking down the stairs from dorm room, these sorority girls approached me about one of my sandz. I said I didn't know where he was and they said "OK LET'S GET HIM!!!" I'm like what??? These ladies grabbed me by my hands and feet and carried me to their car. They called it kidnapping, I called it a fun time. The girl that was driving asked me if I remembered her. I didn't remember her. I didn't remember her from a can of paint but then she begin to talk about the first time we met. It all start coming back. We had

"Miracle Baby"

actually met when I was in the computer lab doing the research about my fraternity. She said she thought I had moved because she didn't see me anymore after that day. "I'm like yea" that's because I was becoming a Made Man. She start laughing and actually offered to buy me food. Anybody who has pledged and became Neos understand the struggle. A mean was well needed starting that I had lost about 30 pounds going through that process. I was pleased that she offered so took I took it. I had barely $20 in my pockets and here it was a soriety girl who was looking good offering me anything. As we ate and rode, I kept making them laugh but the driver was extra with it. When we got back to the campus, she gave her number and said we should kick it. I was like that's cool with me. A couple of days went by and I finally used her number. She said she had a house in Xenia and that she was hosting a party. Ofcourse I gathered all my sandz up and we mobbed over there. It was unlimited drinks, good music and sorority girls. The one girl was flirting and I was flirting back. I believe that night is when we became official. We start dating and it was cool. My sandz and her sandz would kick it on a regular basis, go to the movies, go out to eat, go to parties and more. We start doing everything together. It was always fun to be off campus whenever I could. Instead of being in a dorm room with a roommate I could be at the house with a chick, Oh yea, I'm all in. Here I was fresh off of line, with a car, and a girl who lived off campus. I thought I was winning. She use to bring food to me on campus and buy me things when I needed them. Our friendship was irresistible. Yea, it was all good until her cousin came to the school. Yea my dirty laundry would be aired out very quick. I told yall I was a Neo fresh off of line, so in the campus eyes I was like a celebrity. I kid you not, my facebook went from 1500 to 5000 friends in a matter of days. Girls who never spoke to me was asking to kick it with me. Me and my sandz who were roommates kept a bowl full of condoms on the dresser. Girls would laugh, but they already knew what it was. Now I'm not proud of this, I'm just keeping it 100. I couldn't handle all of the fame, with trying to be in a relationship. Due to all of that, my relationship started to drift, granted we lasted strong for about 2 years going to Chicago, North Carolina, Tennessee, Detroit and other places. After so long of cheating, I was caught up and it was nothing that I could do. To get over my relationship, me and my two niggas drove down to Atlanta and then to Florida. We was smoking, drinking, performing shows and recording music. We were able to meet producers, rappers and a shit load of models. We even hit Jacksonville to holla at my nigga Beze, who been rocking with me since my freshmen year in college. This trip was well needed, but on this trip, I found out one of my aunties was diagnosed with cancer. When I found it, I instantly thought about the time my mom had got cancer and almost died. I remember going up to the hospital after middle school and just sitting in the room watching her breath. She had tubes and needles in her. She was on a breathing machine and non-responsive. I cried for days until she came out of her comma. Although my mom almost died, my auntie pulled through about a year later after she was diagnosed. She is doing well and still as sweet as can be. When I got back from the trip with my homies. I thought it would only be right to reconcile with my ex. We was able to get back cool but things were never the same. I remember riding around campus with my sandz smoking some tree. I see her and some dude by her car. I got out the car and got into dude face. She literally tried to play me and I punched her window. I realized, anytime someone take me out of my character. I can't be around them. So from there, I just us never being a couple again. I had moved on just as well as she did. From time to time, we would kick it but never like before. I had actually start talking back to the girl that I shared prom with, we had known each other since we was teenagers so, I thought it would

"Miracle Baby"

only be right. Although she was many miles away, we started to connect again. At this time I was dibbing and dabbing with the sorority girl but nothing too serious (Just Sex). One day as I'm leaving an Alpha meeting, I get a text stating "I'm pregnant". I thought to myself here we go again, but this time she was actually my girl so I couldn't be mad. When I called her she spoke about her feelings and stated that she didn't know what she was going to do. We would get into heated arguments from time to time and I said some things that I always regret. I told her "I'll pay for an abortion" she would hang up on me and curse me out. Deep down inside I really wanted another child. I wasn't worried, I thought if we made it 3 years we could raise a baby together or at least co parent. I didn't know how I would tell all my family and friends about the pregnancy but I did. Some girls cut me off and some understood. My ex from teenage days stuck by my side and said she was a "ride or die". Nine months later my youngest daughter was born. Debra Darielle Ingham Smith, I was there by her side when she came out. I even cut the umbilical card and signed the birth certificate. I kept saying I didn't do it right the first time, so this time I will do everything according to Gods will. Although I and her mom had been broken up for some time, we shared a precious baby together. Before she gave birth, I had to hang up the phone with my teenage friend who I had just made my girlfriend. She was so solid, she even made 2 trips to Ohio to visit me. The more and more we talked, the more I fell in love. I wanted to do everything right this go around, so I cut off all my lady friends to be just the man she needed. Because my relationship with her was on display, this would ruin my chances of spending time with my youngest daughter. Her mom was very upset and sometimes denied me of being with her.

"I made it"

Oh shoot!!!! I didn't tell yall, before my daughter was born I graduated college. 2 months before she was born actually. It was BIG, my granny came, my cousins came, and my best friend came and guess what, my momma made it too. I graduated wiah a BA in Business Management and Hospitality Management. The day of graduation, I was excited but sad that my oldest daughter couldn't make it to see me walk the stage. At least one of my daughters were there, yea her mom was carrying her and was nice enough to come to my graduation. If I never said thank you "Thank you". A week before graduation I did something most will never do, Yea I slept with one of the baddest professors at the college. She was a Caucasian curly hair thick thang too. When leaving her house the car that I was driving literally caught on fire and blew up. Anyway, after graduating I was working in the college cafeteria as a line cook. My auntie hooked me up with a data entry job in Dayton Ohio. So I quit my café job, and worked in Dayton full time. This job was temporary through Man Power but it paid a lot more then what I was making. After I got off, I would go and see my daughter or go and pick her up. After her mom didn't allow me to see her, and my job assignment was over, I decided to make a decision of moving back to California. Some would say I was crazy or stupid but I believe it was the right decision to make at the moment. I had been in Ohio for 6 years, it was about time to start off fresh in my home town. I

"GOD GOT ME"

“Miracle Baby”

boarded the plane, but when boarding it, I suddenly became sad. I remembered that I was leaving my daughter and that I was going home without seeing my grandpa. My grandpa who had raised me, passed away in his sleep before I graduated college. It was a trip because I was actually in Oakland on a break from school. I had Zaniya in the back seat of my car and my mom in the passenger seat. I took my mom to one of her friend’s house and while I was waiting outside I got a phone call from my cousin Doe. He hit me and said “D”, Emmett passed away. The first thing I could do was hit the gas to the house he was at. My daughter sitting in the chair and not in the car seat with the seat belt on, me driving fast was very unsafe when I think about it now but I was trying to save my grandpa. I left my momma and I didn’t look back. When we got to the house I picked up my daughter and went into the house, my uncle and my cousin approached me. My uncle told me to feel his body, he said “he’s very cold huh”. I just start breaking down and crying. I couldn’t believe I had just lost the only man that fully raised me. He was no blood to me but he took me in as if I was his son. The night before he passed he called me. I remember I was packing and he said, “You coming to get this money I have for you”. I said yea I’ll be there tomorrow, but tomorrow never came for him. Anything you can do today, don’t put it off until tomorrow, because tomorrow is not promised. I broke down and cried on that plane. I actually don’t go to sleep before hopping a plane the next day so I was so tired. I actually fell asleep in tears. When I woke up I was in the city of Oakland, in the state of California. It was sunny and hot. My cousin had actually bought me the ticket and said that it was my graduation gift, Rest in peace Larita, I love you.

When I got home the first place I went was to see my grandmother. It’s like a ritual, after school I go see my grandmother after work I go and see my grandmother, shit, after making a baby I go and see my grandmother. She was so happy to see me. Our relationship is the best I swear she even had a car waiting for me. She bought it from her neighbors but it was a cool little car. I mean literally, it was little, my knees were touching the dash board, but I appreciated the gesture. I tried keeping it in the family and selling it to my uncle but only Lord know what happened to that car. After chatting with grandmother, of course the next stop was to be with my daughter. She was getting big and was in need of a real relationship with her father, which was a major reason of me moving back home. About a week went by and I was enjoying my family and my girlfriend. I was driving in thus black Dodge Charger stepping out to enter the barber shop on Seminary. I saw some dude in a Charger drive by and look at me, then suddenly hit a U-turn. As I’m walking from the Charger, dude screamed out “RELL” and then pulled out a gun. I looked closer and it was one of my niggas from the hood (55th). He was like ‘BRUHHH I THOUGHT YOU WAS THE OTHER RELL, IT WAS ABOUT TO BE CURTAINS”. I was shocked but grateful that I wasn’t the other RELL whoever he was. What’s crazy is from time to time I still see bruh and we chop it up like nothing happened. Dude almost took my head off, Thank GOD for FAVOR. Since then I have had so many close calls to death. One night I was riding from my house after playing 2k on the PS4. I pulled up to the light on 98th in Brookfield, slapping my mixtape “Granny’s Basement” and on Instagram on my phone. When I looked up from swiping my phone. I see a truck on the right side of me, with about 4 black dudes. I looked over at them and when I did, the dude in the passenger seat pointed a big ass gauge at me. I was praying that the light would turn green and when it did, I was out. Them cats turned at the next corner as I kept straight. I was spooked no lie, but GOD always got me. No matter what, that was always my slogan "GOD got my back".

"DownHill"

As you read my story I can sense that someone will see GOD for themselves because he is so real. So remember the friend that I grew up with and took to prom, well, we became more than just girlfriend and boyfriend. One night after smoking with my daughter uncle, I took him to his place in Hayward. Now I don't know if it was the weed or if it was an epiphany, but I do know it was very rare. I saw something very clear and heard things as well, It said "Treat this lady like you never treated a women before, NO, you will not be with your baby mommas, they are not for you". In this I seen my girlfriend and I standing in Christmas sweaters and just having a good time. When I envisioned all this in my mind, I hear my phone ring, it was my cousin and I said "BruhCUZ, she's going to be my wife, I'm not going to cheat and I think I'm in love. My cousin was not ready for this conversation. He was like "OH, OK cool" lol. I was feeling so passionate about this. When I got off the phone with him, I called her up. I don't remember the exact words but I know that I was crying and apologizing for all I had done wrong to her in the past. She was asking if I was OK, I was OK, I just felt deep about this feeling I was having, we exchanged "I Love You" and we got off the phone. When I hung up with her, I start making calls and telling chicks about my relationship and how we couldn't even see each other again. At the time it was the right thing to do, so I wanted to do it right. She told me that she never heard me cry or seen me express my feelings so passionately. I didn't understand where all of this was coming from neither but I stood on what I believed. One night she and I went to the Musiq Soulchild, Donell Jones concert at the Warfield in San Francisco. I knew what I wanted to do, but just didn't know how I would do it. When we got into the Venue and realized how the setting was and where we would sit. I approached the security guard, I told him what I was thinking and he said he would talk it over with the operating coordinator. The security guard was extra cool. After talking to him she was like "What was that all about" I told her that I was trying to perform my music. About 3 minutes later, the security guard came and got me. He introduced me to the coordinator and I told her what I wanted to do. The coordinator walked me to the stage with a lady from the Bay Area radio station. She said this awesome and so sweet. After the act came off of the stage from singing, she introduced me to come on stage. She gave me the mic and I just blew it away. LOL Naw I didn't rap. I told Bri to come up to the stage. I start talking to the crowd briefly about how deeply in love I was with her. Everyone seem to feel each and every word that I spoke. When she got on the stage, I said some words and then dropped to my knees. She was shaking and start crying, I popped the question to her stating "WILL YOU MARRY ME?" she said "YES" and everybody start rooting, clapping and whistling. It was a great feeling when we got off of stage, everybody was saying congratulations and that they wish us well. I was no longer just a boyfriend, I was her fiancé. Although our relationship was sometimes rocky, I thought becoming her fiancé would have brought on a change. Instead of proposing it seems like things went downhill. The love that we had for each other was there but the respect factor left. One day when driving about 45 minutes to her house to give her some flowers. I knocked on her door and she wouldn't answer. So I called her because I was trying to surprise her. She said "Leave or I'll

"Miracle Baby"

"Nothing Last Forever"

call the police". I'm like what the hell I do? We was just talking to each other earlier? She said "You can't jump pop up at my house unannounced". She opened up the window from her room and kept saying "Nigga leave my house". I was wondering why she was being hella disrespectful and angry for. I said "what is the problem"? She said "You are the problem". So I cut out. But I left wondering what the hell had just happen and why was she acting like that. When I got home, she apologized and admitted that she was wrong. Being the forgiven sucker, I was like "It's good". We would be cool again and I would go about my way. Another time, I went to her house while her mom was at work, her sister was at school. We of course had sex, smoked, and then watched Judge Mathis. I remember us playing and snatching each other phones. When I took her phone. She got so defensive and start cursing me out. She start damn near trying to fight me. So when I see this, I start acting like I had broken her code. I was looking in her phone but really didn't see anything. I said to her "Damn that's how you feel"? "Who is this dude"? Real talk yall I didn't even see shit. I sat on the stair and gave her the phone back. She said "I'm sorry" "I only talk to him because I can't talk to you sometimes". I was like wow, so are yall having sex? She said NO "We never did it", but honestly I don't know of any woman who would tell their fiancé about having an affair. From that day she and I relationship became a lot different. She would come to my house for the weekend, we would go to church, have dinner, go out and then she drive back to Vallejo. It was times when she left early due to having attitudes or us arguing. She started to call me out my name, that's when I realized the respect had left the building. She called me bitch ass niggas, Pussy ass niggas, all type of bullshit when she wasn't getting her way. The last time I went to her house, I remember us just arguing. She would be on the phone sounding hella weird. It felt as if somebody was around her or she was doing some freaky shit on the other end of the phone. After hanging up on me, I drove that whole 45 minutes to surprise her, this time really to just talk to her. When I got up to her door, I seen a dude's leg and his shoes on the floor. I knocked, no answer, I rung the door bell, no answer. Her car was parked outside but she wasn't answering. I know it might be a bit creepy now, but she was my fiancée and I didn't understand why she was treating like this. I see someone look through her room window but they wouldn't come to the door. She texted me telling me to leave and not come back. I was getting fed up from her treating me like shit and plus I just had seen some dude shoes on the carpet, which mean this nigga was in there lounging, while I'm outside looking like a sucker. I waited outside in my car for at least 45 minutes but nobody came out the house. I called my homie and he was like "Double, you better than that bruh, just leave." I was trying to see who this nigga was, but apparently they wouldn't come out the house. When I got home I basically was done and over the situation. After this happened and her not wearing her ring on the regular. I knew that our relationship was basically toxic. When I talked to her she was pretty much telling me to deal with it or cut. When we were good, it seemed great, but things got out of hand. After telling her how I felt we didn't talk for a couple of days. She hit me up and expressed how much she missed me. We end up getting back on good terms but we was still rocky. I start drinking heavy due to the strain on our relationship. One day I was in the studio getting drunk and smoking a fat ass blunt, my uncle saw me and told me about myself. I gave him the bottle once I jumped in the car and seen him riding a bike down 55th, but I still was in a depressed state. My hair was falling

“Miracle Baby”

out and I constantly worried. That evening my little cousin was playing in a college basketball game. Me and his brother went to support him, but of course I was hammered in that arena. When we left, me and my fiancé was supposed to be going out to a club together. We was cool the whole day but suddenly things changed. When she got to my house, I greeted her at her car, with a hug and a kiss as a gentle man is supposed to. When I closed her door, she began to walk to my house and then suddenly she stopped and said, “Nigga you couldn’t help me”. I said “you was moving so fast, I couldn’t”. That’s when she called me a “Bitch” and said nigga “I’m leaving”. Mind you, I was still intoxicated from earlier and in my feelings. She actually grabbed her bags from my room that was already in there and proceeded to her car. I’m steady trying to convince her to stay but she wasn’t hearing me. She jumped in her car and drove off. My first thought was to jump in my car and follow her, no matter how intoxicated I was. I chased after her and then she jumped on the freeway, I hopped on the freeway right behind her. She got off on Fruitvale and drove into the plaza and parked in front of Starbucks, where her best friend worked. Her best friend dude was in the car right next to mine waiting for her best friend. I pulled up on the side and hopped out of my car. She was like “Nigga, I don’t want you, leave me alone”. I said ‘you the one told me that you wanted me to go out with yall”. I didn’t understand why she was so mad at me and what I had done. I sat in her car and she was like “get out my fuckin face you bitch ass nigga. I hate you, you bum ass nigga”. I then said “fuck you” and she followed with “fuck you bitch ass nigga”. By this time I got out of her car and slammed her door. Then she goes to say, “I don’t need you nigga, I got someone who can satisfy me, shit I can satisfy myself you bitch ass nigga”. My first thought was ‘Ol Hell Naw”, I walked to her driver side of the car and tried kissing her. She start moving my face with her hands so then I start doing something so stupid that I will forever regret. I can’t believe I did it and I’m still very hurt that it happened. I bit her on her cheek. I was so full of emotion and liquor that I gripped her cheek until my jaw start hurting. She begin to cry and bleed at the same time. I was still in rage. I called her phone looking for my Miami Heat’s hat, but didn’t realize the damage I had caused. I jumped in my car and drove home. Still intoxicated and in rage I couldn’t imagine the pain I had caused her. When I went to church the next day. I got a text on my phone. It was her, she sent a picture of her face and all I could do was cry. I was on the drums feeling like less than human. I was so hurt from the pain I had caused her. I couldn’t believe what I had done. She stated that her mom was going to call the police. After us texting, I get a text from her mom stating how she would kill me if I had ever reached out to her and her family again. Me and her grandmother had a great relationship, but since this incident, I haven’t spoken with her grandmother. God knows my heart and know that I didn’t mean to do this. I couldn’t believe what I had done and still have a hard time processing it today. I had lost my best friend to some foolish act. I was not only hurt from what had happened, but I was scared of the fact that I could be possibly doing some time in jail for Mayhem. Thank God for his grace and mercy. She didn’t press charges nor did she contact the police. Deep down inside, I know that she loved me and knew that I didn’t mean to do that to her. It was totally out of character and much unknown for me to do something like this. After me trying to see her on different occasions, she would first say yes, then she would deny us meeting up. We texted our “I love you still” text from time to time but suddenly I stop getting text back. I haven’t heard from her or seen her since that last time. It was very sad and still plays rapidly in my mind from time to time. I do want to say this to her. I apologize for ever doing that to you. I lost my best friend the day that I lost you. I thank you for not going to the law and giving me a chance. I love you and pray that you are doing great things. I pray that you find it in your heart to forgive me. Maybe one day we will cross paths again, but until then just know that I am truly sorry for hurting you.

For days I stayed in my room and wrote love songs. I was depressed and heart broken. I continued to write music because that was the only outlet I had. One Sunday before going to church, I was hopping out of the shower. When I opened the shower door, the glass from the door instantly shattered. The glass cut me on my feet but as I looked up from feeling the extreme pain from my hand, I noticed my thumb hanging halfway off of my hand. The glass cut one of my tendons, which took feeling away from my thumb. I screamed loud “OH GOD”, and my granny said “Boy what’s wrong with you?” I said “I got cut”. I held my hand up with my left hand. I had put my clothes on with one had by then and my cousin gave me a towel. My cousin rushed me to the hospital. The doctor stated that my tendon had been cut and I would no longer be able to raise my thumb. Which means no telling people “Two Thumbs Up”. I was just glad that it didn’t cut my whole hand off. From this incident, I had to leave work due to not being able to drive or write. I was put on disability but wasn’t getting paid. I went about 3 months without any pay. I got behind on my car note, my rent, my phone bill, and child support. I was very broke, and my bank account was nearly wiped out. I was asking family members to borrow $20 here and there. Thank God my granny looked out for me. She helped me get back on track with all my bills. After being at home for all of these days, I begin to just write music and think of ideas for my clothing line “YOVOY”. As I was watching MTV. I saw a video that caught my attention. I noticed “YOVOY” which is the name of my clothing line tagged in a rappers video. I was very upset and didn’t feel respected. I saw a commercial of Judge Mathis and quickly jotted down the information. When I called the number. I told them my case. They said because I didn’t know the rapper. They wouldn’t be able to take my case. When the lady said that I asked her “What about this scenario with my daughter mom”. I told her how my baby mama put water in my old school Mercedes Benz. When I gave her this spill, she was very pleased with my story. She said she would run it by the producers and get back to me. I said “Thank you very much”. About 2 days passed and I got a phone call. The producer from Judge Mathis called me stating that they loved my story and would like to go farther with it. She said that my daughter mom would have to agree in order to do it. I called her on my work phone and gave her the spill. She stated she would call me back to let me know. I just knew she was going to say no about doing it. So I told the producer I would get back to her. When my baby momma called me back, she said that she was down to doing it, but that she didn’t want her sorority to be displayed.

“Judge Mathis Appearance”

I called the producer back and the process started. I had to get pictures of my car, the estimate price and go down and file small claims. After doing all of this, I got a letter in the mail stating our date to be on the air for the “Judge Mathis” court show. They paid for my plane ticket from Oakland, to Chicago, to Vegas and back. They also paid me to be on their show. I was staying at the Hard Rock Hotel in Downtown Chicago. They fed me and gave me limousine rides from, and to the air ports. A man was standing by baggage claim with a sign that read “Darrell Smith”

“Miracle Baby”

when I got off of the plane. I couldn’t believe that I was really about to be on television. They had me in a room with bulb lights going around the mirrors. They begin to put make up on my face while they asked me questions. I was feeling some type of way about the makeup but they explained to me why they had to do this. For recording purposes and the lighting and some other stuff. They put a mic on my shirt and the box in my back pocket so that the sound would be very clear for the audience as well as for the TV viewers. I walked out to do the first walk through, as I walk to the podium, my daughter mom comes outs on the left side of the building. It was pretty weird , they had us walk in front of the podium while there was a bunch of people behind us in the audience. They made us turn around and go back out. I’m thinking “I made it Big Granny, Momma, Grandmother “ LOL. When we finally was called back to enter the room, we stood and waited for Judge Mathis. As he came out I’m thinking “Here we go” “Game time”. I pleaded my case and gave my story as best as I could. I won’t say everything that was said but just know, I walked out of there $5000 richer. At the end of us pleading our cases, I was able to hold my daughter. It was a very bitter sweet feeling due to the whole situation. I was so happy to see my daughter and to hold her in my arms again. He mom had been keeping her away from me, not answering phone calls or text messages. Granted they live in Ohio and I live in California, but the efforts were always denied by her and still is honestly. Because of some of the things that my daughter mom was saying along with my daughter grandmother, swearing at me and talking a bunch of chaos, the people quickly escorted me out of the building. They made me go a different way and escorted me through the garage right into the limousine. It was a good experience but I just wanted more time with my daughter. They sent me straight to the airport to catch my flight for Vegas. I went to Vegas and had a ball with my family. In life sometimes your adversity will build your character. If it wasn’t for me getting hurt, I probably would have never called Judge Mathis. I was always on the go and moving so fast. Being down helped me to slow down and create an opportunity not only for me but for my daughter mom as well. She was also paid for attending on the TV show. They gave her, my daughter and my daughter grandmother a free room and food. On top of that my daughter was able to see her father again. It was a Win Win, if you ask me. Doing this taught me a lot about the industry and how the entertainment is ran.

When my grandmother seen me on TV she cried. All of my family was shocked and I received so many phone calls and text messages. People were writing in my DM’s (direct messages) on all of my social media sites. I still get people talking to me about my appearance on that show. A lady came up to me and asked me for my autograph. I didn’t think anything of it but I took a picture and signed my name for her. A little after my appearance, I decided that with some of that money I wanted to put rims on my car. I purchased some rims off of craigslist. I bought some 22 inch rims and some 20’s. These rims were raw. My 22’s were chrome and my 20’s were all black. I have a white Chevy Malibu, with the window tinted and TV in the dash. It was only right that I put the black 20’ rims on it. I took my car to 55th tire shop in East Oakland right on International, for those who are familiar with the town. It was about 5:30 or 6pm. When I pulled up they were drinking, smoking weed and chatting. They said they didn’t feel like putting my rims on but if I could bring it back in the morning, it would be a lot better. When the next day came, I went to work as normal and then headed to the tire shop. The same guys were there, although it was the morning, they were still smoking and drinking. They put my rims on my car and I was juiced (excited). When I hopped on the freeway, I noticed a wobbly sound on my car.

The car started shaking and before I knew it, my tire was flying across highway 880, almost bouncing over to the oncoming traffic. My car dropped with an impact and suddenly my back and neck was stiff. Luckily, they had someone on the freeway that rescued people on a regular. The man was able to find my tire on the interstate. He waited with me until my tow truck came

"Rainy Dayz"

and got me. When I got back to the shop, the owner stated that they didn't put the right bolts on my car and that was the cause of the tire coming off. The first thing that jumped in my mind was "Thank God" I didn't die. When I said that he looked at me dumb founded. Suddenly a light bulb struck in my brain "Law Suit". For the next year I would be doing physical therapy and going to the chiropractor for my neck and back. The doctors stated that one of my disc were cracked in my neck and my back has s deficiency now. After all I'm just thankful that no was injured and I made it out alive. This still plays back in my head along with every other obstacle that I had to overcome. I instantly got me a lawyer and filed a law suit. Not only did it ruin my body but traumatically it has played a toll on me. Now not everything is bad in my life. I have a great family and great moments but this book is to inspire those who are going through similar situations, and just need some advice about getting out. As I'm writing this, I am very sadden today. My youngest daughter Debra Darielle, turned 6 today, but because her mom is upset about me not signing her passport, she won't even let me talk to her. I haven't spoken with my daughter since I left Ohio 2 months ago, after purchasing my first house actually. It's hard enough not to be able to see her. Any person who keep their kids away from their parent is cruel, unkind, selfish and vindictive, but I'll let GOD handle that situation.

One night me and my cousin was chopping it up and decided that we wanted to drink due to her getting me a security job. Although it probably wasn't the right thing to do on a weekday. We was celebrating for her putting me on for this security company. We were driving down 77th and MacArthur in East Oakland mind you. I have tinted windows, a white car and black rims. I look to the left and witness some Mexican guys with guns in their hands. They looked like they had army guns and loading them in a truck. I tapped my cousin and told her to "look over there". I stared as one of the Mexican man caught my eyes. I kept driving thinking nothing of it. As we are driving, we are talking about how crazy Oakland is and how I was ready to get the hell out of this town. "These Niggas just out here with army guns, like its Iraq or something", my cousin start laughing. As we approached the Beacon gas station on the right of us, I stopped at the red traffic light. As we are waiting for the light to change to green, I looked out of my side mirror and notice that same big ass truck that the dudes were loading up with guns. They were riding real close almost hitting my side mirror. As I see someone lean out of the truck, I see him pull out a gun and start shooting. POW,POW,POW.... It was about 10 shots that rung, but I only heard 3 hit my car. When I see the gun, I instantly start leaning to my cousin side and ducking my body, as I turned the car right. I was leaning so far over, almost covering my cousin body so that she wouldn't get hit. I speed off and hit the freeway going about 60 mph on a residential street. When we got off the freeway, I hopped out at the liquor store in San Leandro to look at my body and the car. I felt my body only because my adrenaline was very high and couldn't feel

"Thank God for the Miracle Baby"

anything. Thank God I didn't get hit at all because they were so close. My car was hit 3 times almost in a line as I thought from hearing the impact of the bullets. One bullet hole in the nose of my car, the second in my driver door and the third in the back door. It happened so fast, but all I could do was thank God that we were safe. No one was hurt, one bullet even got through my front door but I believe it hit my seat. That was supposed to be my head, my stomach and my leg but God said it aint so. Can't tell me that he wasn't looking out for me. After this incident, my family thought it would be best for me to get into another car. That's when I end up getting into my all White 2015 Dodge Charger, Big Body. This thang was so powerful and as comfortable as can be. I was on cloud 99 riding around in my charger. I know, I know, I'm speaking as if it was the past, will it is. Because one morning after leaving my grave yard shift as a Security in Millbrae, at the Aloft Hotel. Around 5am, it was raining and storming very hard. It was actually hailing and the wind was blowing so hard, from left to right. I'm listening to my gospel music and just praying to get home safe. Suddenly my car start drifting to the right, mind you I am on the Bay Bridge. Great thing, no one was on the highway with me, well at least while this was happening. As my car start drifting to the right side of the highway, I pull it back and start moving forward again. About 9 seconds later, the car started to slide and drift to the left. This time trying to pull it back was impossible. I hit the brake, it slid, I turned my steering wheel, it kept sliding, and all I can do now is just ask God to keep me protected. BAM!!!!! My car ran into the wall with the air bags instantly being released, and smoke appearing very high. The airbags all around the car came out, ones that I didn't even know my car had. I jumped out of the car in the pouring rain on the side of the Bay Bridge as cars were passing me. I was so crushed man, I contacted my granny and my auntie. They were most concerned about me and both stated that a car can always be replaced but not me. A police came and hit my car out of the way from oncoming traffic. He let me sit in his truck, but I was thinking like "Why Lord", why things keep happening to me. He said "Why Not" so I couldn't even complain. I walked out of that accident with no scratches and no broken bones. Thank You God again. My car was considered totaled out. Because I didn't have gap insurance I'm still paying that car off even without having it. No matter how difficult life may be, remember someone would love to be in your shoes. I am currently helping my mom overcome her struggles. She was diagnosed with cancer and it has took a toll on her body. This experience makes me put things into perspective. Every day we as humans are chasing a check, money, currency, mula, dineros, pasos, but at the end of the day, when you are in these situations that you all have read throughout the literature, money can't buy you a blessed life. Money can't buy favor, money can't buy God's grace and mercy. Cherish the things that you have YES, but most importantly cherish the people that you share life with. When my grandmother took sick and had a stroke, I remember when she was in the hospital bed and the words that she spoke so sweet. She said "God will do what he said he'll do". That blew me and my uncle's mind, while we were visiting her. She has been through everything from almost dying multiple times, to her witnessing people die and she still keeping her faith strong. My uncle is doing time now, my little cousin has a couple of years in jail, my brother has been sentenced life, but through it all they have love, and God is love. They are not going through these experiences alone because as long as I am alive, I will be with them. Yes all this is very

“Miracle Baby”

traumatic for me, Yes it’s painful at times but after all that is said and done, this is a life of a “Miracle Baby”.

I wouldn’t be right if I didn’t shout out a couple of people that inspired me to do this.

Shout out to:

My Grandmother Clarene Smith

My Mother Deborah Smith

My Granny Helen Raymond

My Grandpa Emmett Rhodes

My Pastor Percy Winn

My Auntie Elaine Winn

My Auntie Marilyn Adams

My Big Cousin Kimberly Adams

My Cousin/ Uncle Derrick (Dirty D) Knockum

My Uncle Henry (Peedee) Smith

My Kids Zaniya and Debra Smith

My Family and Friends that believed in me.

I love each and every one of you. Last but of course not least I give a special thanks to Jesus Christ for giving me this opportunity and ability to follow my dreams.

“Miracle Baby”

www.ingramcontent.com/pod-product-compliance
Ingram Content Group UK Ltd.
Pitfield, Milton Keynes, MK11 3LW, UK
UKHW041901190726
13854UKWH00003B/1028

9 781387 367771